Country Candy Sweets & Treats

Suzie & TK Cornman

Table of Contents

Cakes & Cookies   7

Breads & Muffins   42

Candy   61

This & That   83

Index   96

Why We Need Recipes
-Author Unknown-

I guessed the pepper,
    the soup was too hot.
I guessed the water,
    it dried in the pot.
I guessed the salt,
    and what do you think?
We did nothing else
    the whole day but drink.
I guessed the sugar,
    the sauce was too sweet,
And so by my guessing,
    I spoiled the treat.
And now I guess nothing,
    for cooking by guess
Is sure to result
    in a terrible mess.

-Happy Creating! Suzie and Kat

Cakes
&
Cookies

Wacky Cake

2 C. Water
2 C. Sugar   2 T. Vinegar
3 C. Flour   2 T. Vanilla
¾ C. Oil   1 tsp. Baking Soda
¾ C. Cocoa   1 tsp. Salt

Blend together the sugar, vinegar, oil, water, and vanilla. Add in the flour, cocoa, salt, and baking soda. Mix well. Pour into a greased and floured pan. Bake at 350 until a toothpick comes out clean.

*A Depression era cake that is totally vegan.

Marian's Chocolate Sheet Cake

2 C. Flour, sifted
2 C. Sugar
1 C. Water
½ C. Sour Cream
2 sticks Butter

4 T. Baking Cocoa
1 tsp. Baking Soda
½ tsp. Salt
1 Egg

Frosting

1 lb. Powdered Sugar
1 stick Butter
6 T. Milk

4 T. Baking Cocoa
1 ½ tsp. Vanilla Extract
½ C. Chopped Walnut (optional)

Cook cocoa, butter, and water together and bring to a boil. Mix flour, sugar, and salt together. When cocoa mixture has boiled, remove from heat and add to flour mixture. Add sour cream, soda, and egg. Mix well. Pour into a greased 9 inch x 13 inch baking sheet. Batter will be very thin. Bake at 350 until toothpick comes out clean.

For frosting: Cook cocoa, milk, and butter over low heat until bubbling. Pour over powdered sugar. Add vanilla and walnuts, if desired. Mix until frosting is smooth.

Frost the cake while still warm.

Old Fashioned Coffee Cake

4 C. Flour

2 C. Brown Sugar, packed

2 C. Buttermilk

1 ½ C. Oil

1 ½ C. Sugar

3 large Eggs

1 T. + 1 tsp. Baking Powder

2 tsp. Nutmeg

2 tsp. Cinnamon

2 tsp. Baking Soda

¾ tsp. Salt

12 oz. Chopped Walnuts (optional)

Blend flour, sugar, salt, nutmeg, oil, and nuts, if desired, together. Mix until batter is crumbly then set aside 1 ½. C. of crumble mixture. Add into remaining mixture the baking soda, baking powder, eggs, and buttermilk. Mix gently. Pour into two greased and floured 11 inch x 17 inch pans. Sprinkle crumb topping evenly over batter. Bake at 350 until a toothpick comes out clean.

*Can be eaten as is or you can add Powdered Sugar Glaze (pg. 89) to top.

Christmas Pumpkin Cake

3 ¼ C. Pumpkin/1 large can

3 C. Sugar

3 C. Flour

1 ½ C. Oil

4 Eggs, slightlybeaten

1 T. Baking Powder

1 T. Baking Soda

1 T. Cinnamon

Nuts or Raisins optional

Blend sugar, flour, baking powder, cinnamon, and salt. Mix well. Add oil and mix until dry ingredients are moistened. Add pumpkin, egg, and nuts/raisins if desired. Mix until well blended. Pour batter into 3 lightly greased pans with parchment paper in the bottom for easy removal and level out. Bake at 350 until light brown or until toothpick comes out clean. Cool on ricks. Turn out cakes. Layer and top with vanilla or cream cheese frosting (pg. 89).

Mom Hudson's Apple Dump Cake

2 C. Sugar	2 Eggs
2 C. Flour	1 tsp. Baking Soda
½ C. Oil	1 tsp. Cinnamon
1 can Apple Pie Filling	1 tsp. Vanilla Extract
1 C. Chopped Nuts (optional)	

Pour apples into a large bowl and chop into small pieces. Mix the apples, sugar, eggs, and oil together by hand. Mix the dry ingredients together then add to the apple mixture. Mix well. Put into a greased 13 inch x 9 inch pan. Bake at 350 until a toothpick comes out clean.

Apple Crisp

1 C. Oats	½ tsp. Cinnamon
½ C. Brown Sugar	¼ tsp. Salt
¼ C. Flour	⅛ tsp. Nutmeg
4 T. Butter	1 can Apple Pie Filling

Blend oats, sugar, flour, salt and spices together. Cut in Butter and mix until crumbly. Spread filling into a pie pan or square baking dish. Sprinkle the crumb mixture over top. Bake at 350 until it's light brown and bubbly on top.

Fried Pies

2 C. Flour   1 tsp. Salt
⅓ C. Cold Water   Pie Filling
½ C. Shortening

Blend flour, salt, shortening, and water until it is a dough. This is a tough dough. Roll out on a flour-covered board to about a ¼ inch thick. Cut into big squares or circles. Fill the middle of the shapes with pie filling. Bring the opposite edges of the dough together and press the edges to seal pies. Fry in hot oil until golden brown.

*Canned pie filling can be used or you can make your own. The recipe for Pie Filling is on page 93.
*Cinnamon and sugar can be sprinkled onto the pies, especially if making apple.

Cheese Cake

5 pkg. (8 oz) Cream Cheese	3 T. Flour
1 ¾ C. Sugar	½ tsp. Lemon Juice
3 Eggs	

Sour Cream Topping

1 pt. Sour Cream	1 tsp. Vanilla Extract
½ C. Sugar	

Leave out the cream cheese and eggs for 1 hour.
Preheat oven to 500 degrees.
Use a 10 inch spring pan.

Beat cream cheese, sugar, flour, juice, and vanilla together. Beat in eggs one at a time till well combined. Pour cream cheese mixture into pan. Bake for 10 minutes at 500. Reduce temp to 250 and bake until top cracks a little. When cake is done, take out and let set for 30 minutes. When the cake is cool, pour sour cream topping on top of it. Bake at 450 for 8 minutes. Take out and let cool.

No Bake Cheese Cake

8 oz. pkg. Cream Cheese, softened
1 can Sweetened Condensed Milk
$\frac{1}{3}$ C. Reconstituted Lemon Juice
1 tsp. Vanilla Extract
1 Pie Crust   Pie filling (optional)

Beat cream cheese, milk, and vanilla together with electric mixer. Add in juice slowly. Mix until mixture is smooth. Pour into pie crust. Chill. Top with pie filling to eat.

Carrot Cake

3 C. Carrots, ground/grated	1 tsp. Baking Soda
2 C. Sugar	1 tsp. Salt
2 C. Flour	½ tsp. Allspice
1 ½ C. Oil	1 C. Nuts (optional)
4 Eggs	

Blend eggs, sugar, oil, and carrots together. Add in the dry ingredients and nuts, if desired. Mix well. Bake at 350 until toothpick comes out clean.

No Bake Fruit Cake

2 lbs. Walnuts	2 lbs. Marshmallows
2 lbs. Brazil Nuts	2 lbs. Glazed Maraschino Cherries
2 lbs. Almonds	2 lbs. Glazed Pinapple
2 lbs. Pecans	2 12 oz. boxes Vanilla Wafers
2 lbs. Dates	1 can Evaporated Milk

Chop all nuts and cherries into small pieces. Crush vanilla wafers into crumbs. Mix nuts and fruits into crumbs. Cook marshmallows and milk until melted together. Pour liquid over the crumb mixture and mix until well blended. Press firmly into wax-lined loaf pans. Let set.

Easy Pound Cake

1 pkg. Yellow Cake Mix	½ C. Water
½ C. Oil	1 pkg. Instant Vanilla
Pudding	

Blend ingredients together. Mix well. Bake in loaf pan at 350 until toothpick comes out clean.

Pecan Pie

1 C. Dark Corn Syrup	4 T. Butter, melted
½ C. Sugar	1 tsp. Vanilla Extract
3 Eggs	1 C. Pecans, broken

Cook sugar and syrup until mixture thickens. Beat eggs together slowly. Add syrup mixture, beating constantly. Add butter, vanilla, and nuts. Pour into unbaked pie crust. Bake 10 minutes at 450. Reduce temp to 300 and bake for 35 minutes. Let Cool.

Fudge Brownie Pie

2 Eggs	$\frac{1}{3}$ C. Baking Cocoa
1 C. Sugar	1 tsp. Vanilla Extract
½ C. Butter, melted	½ C. Nuts (optional)
½ C. Flour	

Blend eggs, sugar, and butter together. Add flour, cocoa, and salt. Mix well. Add vanilla. Pour into a bottom greased pie pan. Bake at 350 until a toothpick comes out clean. Let cool.
*Cut into wedges and top with ice cream and chocolate sauce; serve warm.

Chocolate Pudding

2 C. Milk
$\frac{2}{3}$ C. Sugar
¼ C. Baking Cocoa
2 Egg Yolks, slightly beaten

2 T. Cornstarch
1 tsp. Vanilla Extract
$\frac{1}{8}$ tsp. Salt

Blend sugar, cornstarch, salt, and cocoa in medium saucepan. Combine milk and egg yolk; gradually stir into sugar mixture. Cook over medium heat, stirring constantly until mixture thickens and boils. Boil for 1 minute, stirring constantly. Remove from heat; stir in butter and vanilla. Pour into a bowl. Chill.

Vanilla Pudding

2 C. Milk	2 T. Butter
$\frac{1}{3}$ C. Sugar	2 T. Vanilla Extract
2 Egg Yolks, slightly beaten	$\frac{1}{8}$ tsp. Salt
2 T. Cornstarch	

Blend sugar, cornstarch, and salt in medium suacepan. Combine milk and egg yolks; gradually add into sugar mixture. Cook over medium heat, stirring constantly unitl mixture thickens and boils. Boil for 1 minute, stirring constantly. Remove from heat, stir in butter and vanilla. Pour into a bowl. Chill.

Butterscotch Pudding

2 C. Milk	2 T. Butter, softened
$\frac{2}{3}$ C. Brown Sugar, packed	1 tsp. Vanilla Extract
2 Egg Yolks, slightly beaten	$\frac{1}{8}$ tsp. Salt
2 T. Cornstarch	

Blend sugar, cornstarch, and salt in medium suacepan. Combine milk and egg yolks; gradually add into sugar mixture. Cook over medium heat, stirring constantly unitl mixture thickens and boils. Boil for 1 minute, stirring constantly. Remove from heat, stir in butter and vanilla. Pour into a bowl. Chill.

Oreo Cookie Dessert

1 pkg. Chocolte Pudding   **1 tub Cool Whip Topping**
Oreo Cookies

Cook the pudding according to box instructions. Line bottom of pan with whole Oreos. Pour half of the pudding over Oreos. Cover pudding with whole Oreos. Blend the rest of the pudding with half of the Cool Whip topping, making a mousse. Cover Oreos with mousse. Chill until set. Serve with Cool Whip on top.

Chocolate Butter Cookies

1 ½ C. Flour	¼ C. Baking Cocoa
½ C. Sugar	1 Egg Yolk
¾ C. Butter, softened	1 tsp. Almond Extract

Beat eggs and butter together for 2-3 minutes until fluffy. Blend in almond extract. Add flour and cocoa. Mix well. Bake at 350 until the edges are firm. Let cool.

Chocolate Crinkle Cookies

2 $\frac{1}{3}$ C. Flour	2 tsp. Vanilla Extract
2 C. Sugar	2 tsp. Baking Powder
¾ C. Oil	½ tsp. Salt
¾ C. Baking Cocoa	Powdered Sugar
4 Eggs	

Combine sugar and oil. Add cocoa. Mix well. Beat in eggs and vanilla. Combine flour, baking powder, and salt; add to cocoa mixture. Mix well. Cover and chill for 6 hours. Shape dough into 1 inch balls. Roll in powdered sugar. Place on greased baking sheet. Bake at 350 until almost no indentation remains when touched. Let cool.

Sugar Cookies

3 ½ C. Flour

1 C. Sugar

¾ C. Shortening

2 Eggs

$\frac{1}{3}$ C. Milk

3 tsp. Baking Powder

½ tsp. Salt

½ tsp. Vanilla

Cream shortening, eggs, milk, vanilla, and sugar together. Add in flour, baking powder, and salt. Mix well. Roll out portions of dough on a floured board to 1/8 inch thick. Cut dough into desired shapes. Put dough shapes onto baking sheets. Sprinkle with sugar/colored sugar or leave plain for powdered sugar /frosted . Bake at 350 until edges are golden brown. Let cool. Plain cookies can be dusted with powdered sugar or decorated with frosting.

* This recipe is over 100 years old and was from a handful and pinch recipe.

Chocolate Sugar Cookies

1 ⅓ C. Flour
½ C. Baking Cocoa
¾ C. Sugar
1 Stick Butter/Margarine
1 Egg

1 tsp. Vanilla Extract
1 tsp. Baking Soda
1 tsp. Baking Powder
¼ tsp. Salt

Cream butter, sugar, eggs, and vanilla together. Mix in cocoa, baking soda and powder, salt and flour. Mix well. Roll out dough on flour cocoa mixture dusted board and cut into shapes. Put onto baking sheets. Sprinkle dough with sugar or leave plain to be frosted or dusted with powdered sugar. Bake at 350 until sides are firm. Let the plain ones cool before decorating with frosting.

Cinnamon Refrigerator Cookies

4 ½ C. Flour   3 Eggs
1 ½ C. Shortening   1 T. Hot Water
1 C. Sugar   2 tsp. Cinnamon
1 C. Brown Sugar   1 tsp. Baking Soda

Mix sugars, cinnamon, baking soda, water, eggs, and shortening together. Add in flour. Mix well. Form dough into rolls 2 inches in diameter. Refrigerate until firm. Cut dough into 1/8 in thick slices. Bake at 350 until light brown. Sprinkle with cinnamon sugar. Dough will keep 3 to 4 weeks

Melting Moments

½ lb. Butter   1 C. Flour
5 ½ T. Powdered Sugar   ¾ C. Cornstartch
Icing: ¾ C. Powdered Sugar 1 ½ T. Orange Juice

Cream butter with powdered sugar and cornstarch. Add flour. Mix well. Roll dough into balls the size of nickels. Bake at 350 until light brown. Cool. Mix powdered sugar and juice toether well to make icing. Dot the tops of cookies with icing.

Tea Cakes

2 ¼ C. Flour   1 tsp. Vanilla Extract
1 C. Shortening   ½ tsp. Salt
½ C. Powdered Sugar   ¾ C. Nuts (optional)

Cream shortening and powder sugar then gradually add in flour, salt, vanilla, and/or nuts. Roll into balls and bake at 350 until the bottoms are light brown. Roll cookies in powdered sugar while hot.

Ginger Snaps

2 C. Flour	1 tsp. Baking Soda
1 C. Sugar	1 tsp. Cinnamon
¾ C. Shortening	½ tsp. Ground Clove
¼ C. Molasses	½ tsp. Ginger
1 Egg	½ tsp. Salt

Cream shortening and sugar together. Add in molasses and egg. Mix well. Add in flour, baking soda, cinnamon, clove, ginger, and salt. Form into 1 inch balls. Roll balls in sugar. Place on greased baking sheet. Bake at 350 until cookies are firm. Let stand 1 minute before removing from baking sheet.

Shortbread Cookies

3 C. Flour
1 ½ C. Shortening
¾ C. Powdered Sugar

½ tsp. Baking Powder
¼ tsp. Salt

Mix together baking powder, salt, sugar, shortening, and flour. Break into 1 inch balls and place on baking sheet. Press a thumbprint into each ball. Bake at 350 for 5-8 minutes until the edges are light brown. Fill cookies with warm fudge frosting (p. 89)

Chocolate Shortbread Cookies

½ C. Butter (no substitutes), softened

½ C Flour

¼ C. Powdered Sugar

1 to 2 T. Baking Cocoa

1 tsp. Vanilla Extract

Cream the butter. Add in the vanilla and mix well. Blend flour, sugar, and cocoa; add to creamed mixture. Knead until dough holds together, takes about 3 minutes. Pat into 9x4 rectangle. Cut into 2 inch by 1-1/2 inch strips. Place 1 inch apart on ungreased baking sheet. Prick with a fork. Bake at 350 until sides are firm.

Pecan Sandies

4 C. Flour

2 C. Butter

1 C. Powdered Sugar

2 T. Water

4 tsp. Vanilla Extract

2 C. Chopped Pecans

Cream butter, sugar, water, and vanilla together. Add in flour and nuts. Mix well. Roll dough in 1 inch balls. Place on baking sheet then flatten with fingers. Bake at 350 until cookies are light brown. When cookies have cooled, dip one end in melted chocolate.

Thumbprint Cookies

1 ¾ C. Flour
¾ C. Powdered Sugar
½ C. Butter
1 Egg

1 tsp. Vanilla Extract
¼ tsp. Salt
Any Jelly or Jam

Cream butter, powdered sugar, salt, egg, and vanilla together. Add in flour. Mix well. Roll dough into balls and put on baking sheet. Press a thumbprint well into the center of each cookie. Bake at 350 until edges of cookies are light brown. Let cool slightly. Add a dab of jelly/jam to the top of the cookie. Let sit to set.

Snickerdoodles

2 ¾ C. Flour	2 tsp. Cream of Tartar
1 ½ C. Sugar	2 tsp. Cinnamon
1 C. Shortening, softened	1 tsp. Baking Soda
2 Eggs, Unbeaten	½ tsp. Salt

Sift flour, cream of tartar, baking soda, salt, and cinnamon together. Cream shortening, sugar, and eggs until light and fluffy. Beat in flour mixture. Chill until the dough is easy to handle. Form dough into balls and place 2 inches apart on ungreased baking sheet. Flatten balls with bottom of glass dipped in sugar and cinnamon. Bake at 350 until light brown.

Chocolate Chip Cookies

2 ½ C. Flour
1 C. Shortening
1 C. Brown Sugar
¾ C. Sugar
3 Eggs

1 ½ tsp. Vanilla Extract
1 tsp. Baking Soda
1 tsp. Salt
3 C. Chocolate Chips/Candy

Blend sugar, eggs, vanilla, and shortening together. Add in flour, baking soda, salt, and chips/candy. Mix well. Bake at 350 until the edges are light brown.

*Cookies can be spread on a baking sheet to make bars. Three types of chocolate can be used to make a better tasting cookie.

Peanut Butter Cookies

1 C. Flour	¼ C. Peanut Butter,Heaping
$\frac{1}{3}$ C. Shortening	1 tsp. Baking Powder
$\frac{1}{3}$ C. Sugar	½ tsp. Salt
$\frac{1}{3}$ C. Brown Sugar	½ tsp. Vanilla Extract
1 Egg	Chocolate Kisses/Buttons

Cream sugar and shortening together. Add in peanut butter and egg. Mix well. Blend in flour, baking powder, salt, and vanilla. Mix well. Drop onto baking sheet by tsp. Flatten with fork in parallel design or make a thumbprint in center. Bake at 350 until golden brown. For the thumbprint cookies, put chocolate kisses/buttons on top of cookie just as the cookies are turning brown.

Pinwheel Galaxy Cookies

1 ½ C. Flour   ¾ tsp. Salt
1 C. Sugar   ½ tsp. Baking Soda
½ C. Shortening   1 tsp. Vanilla Extract
1 Egg   3 oz. Chocolate (if desired)

Blend shortening, sugar, vanilla, and egg together. Add in flour, salt, and baking soda. Mix well. Roll out dough between two sheets of plastic wrap, vanilla and chocolate individually. Put chocolate on top of vanilla. Roll the dough into a pinwheel log. Refrigate dough for at least 30 minutes. Slice dough into ½ inch pieces and place on baking sheet. Bake at 350 until light brown.

*Dust with powdered sugar for galaxy cookies.

Devil's Food Cookies

3 ½ C. Flour	¼ C. Water
2 C. Sugar	2 tsp. Vanilla Extract
1 C. Shortening	1 tsp. Baking Soda
1 C. Baking Cocoa	1 tsp Salt
2 Eggs	1 C. Nuts (optional)
1 ½ C. Sourmilk or Buttermilk	

Beat eggs and water with fork until blended. Blend in sugar, flour, cocoa, vanilla, and salt. Add in shortening. Mix well. Chill dough for 1 hour. Place by teaspoonful onto baking sheet 2 inches apart. A nut can be placed in the center if each cookie if desired.
Bake at 350 until edges are firm to touch.

*Can be made as cupcakes. Just don't overcook them.

No Bake Cookies

1 ½ C. Oats   ¼ C. Peanut Butter
1 C. Sugar   2 T. Baking Cocoa
½ stick Margarine   ½ tsp. Vanilla Exract
¼ C. Milk

Combine sugar, margarine, milk, and cocoa together in saucepan. Bring to a boil. Add peanut butter, vanilla, and oats. Mix well. Drop onto baking sheet in spoonfuls. Let cool to set.

Vanilla Wafers

1 ¼ C. Flour   2 T. Milk
$\frac{2}{3}$ C. Shortening   2 tsp. Vanilla Extract
½ C. Sugar   1 tsp. Baking Powder
1 Egg   ¼ tsp. Salt

Blend shortening, sugar, egg, milk, and vanilla together. Add flour, baking powder, and salt. Mix well. Drop by teaspoon onto baking sheet. Bake at 350 until golden brown.

Cinnamon Oatmeal Cookies

1 C. Margarine

1 ¾ C. Flour

1 ½ C. Oats

1 C. Sugar

½ C. Brown Sugar

1 Egg

1 tsp. Vanilla Extract

1 tsp. Baking Soda

1 tsp. Cinnamon

Cream margarine, sugar, brown sugar, vanilla and egg together. Add flour, oats, soda, and cinnamon. Mix well. Roll into balls, flatten with glass dipped in cinnamon and sugar mixture. Bake at 350 until the edges are golden brown.

Banana Oatmeal Cookies

1 ¾ C. Oats	1 tsp. Salt
1 ½ C. Flour	¾ tsp Cinnamon
1 C. Sugar	½ tsp. Baking Powder
¾ C. Shortening	¼ tsp. Nutmeg
1 Egg	½ C. Nuts (optional)
2 Ripe Bananas, mashed	

Cream sugar, shortening, egg, and bananas together. Mix in baking powder, salt, cinnamon, nutmeg, oats, and nuts (optional). Drop by teaspoon onto a baking sheet. Bake at 350 for 15 minutes until cookie is firm to the touch.

Chocolate Chip Oatmeal Cookies

3 C. Oats

1 ¼ C. Margarine

1 ½ C. Flour

¾ C. Brown Sugar

½ C. Sugar

1 Egg

1 tsp. Vanilla Extract

1 tsp. Baking Soda

1 tsp. Cinnamon

½ tsp. Salt

$\frac{1}{8}$ tsp. Nutmeg

2 C. Chocolate Chips

Cream margarine, egg, vanilla, and sugars together. Add flour, baking soda, salt, cinnamon, nutmeg, and oats. Mix well. Blend in chips. Roll into balls and place on baking sheets. Bake at 350 until edges golden brown.

Rollo Cookies

Flour   ½ tsp. Salt
vn Sugar   ½ tsp. Baking Soda
tening   1 C. Chopped Pecans
                                1 pkg. of Rollos
lla Extract

town sugar, and shortening together. Add flour, pecans. Mix well. Make silver dollar shapes in palm with dough. Place a Rollo, top down, on dough and wrap dough around it. Place on baking sheet. Bake for 350 until light brown.

Chocolate Marshmallow Drops

1 ¾ C. Flour
1 C. Sugar
½ C. Baking Cocoa
½ C. Shortening, softened
½ C. Milk
1 Egg, beaten

½ tsp. Salt
1 tsp. Vanilla Extract
½ tsp. Salt
½ C. Nuts (optional)
24 large Marshmallows

Cut marshmallows horizontally. Sift flour with baking powder, salt, and cocoa. Mix shortening, sugar, egg, and vanilla together until creamy. Blend in flour mixture alternately with the milk. Stir in nuts, if desired. Drop by spoonfuls onto greased baking sheet. Bake at 350 until edges are firm. Remove from oven for about 4 minutes or until cookies are done and marshmallow is softened. Cool and spread cocoa glaze on top of each cookie.

Cocoa Glaze

2 C. Powdered Sugar   4 to 6 T. Hot Milk
½ C. Baking Cocoa

Sift powdered sugar with cocoa. Gradually stir in hot milk until soft enough for glaze to spread easily on cookies.

My Recipe

Breads & Muffins

Raisin Bars & Muffins

2 C. Flour   1 tsp. ground clove
1 C. Raisins   1 tsp. allspice
1 C. Sugar   1 tsp. Cinnamon
½ C. Shortening   1 tsp. Baking Soda
1 Egg   Nuts (optional)

Boil raisins in 2 cups water until 1 cup of water remains. Add sugar, egg, shortening, cloves, allspice, cinnamon, baking soda, flour, and nuts. Mix well. Pour onto a greased baking sheet. Bake on 350 until toothpick comes out clean. Ice with Powdered Sugar Glaze (pg. 89)

Raisin Bread

5 ½ to 6 C. Flour
1 C. Skim Milk, warmed
$\frac{1}{3}$ C. Water, warmed
½ C. Sugar

2 Eggs, lightly beatened
2 Active Dry Yeast .25 oz. pkg.
6 T. Butter, softened
1 ¼ tsp. Salt

Filling:

2-3 C. Raisins
1 C. Water
1 Egg, beaten

$\frac{1}{3}$ C. Apple juice/cider
1 T. Cinnamon

Dissolve yeast in water; let stand for 5 minutes. Add 2 C. flour, milk, eggs, sugar, butter, and salt. Mix well. Add flour until a soft dough is formed. Knead on floured surface until dough is smooth and elastic. Place in bowl coated with nonstick cooking spray, turning once to grease top. Cover and let dough rise in warm place until doubled; takes about 1 hour. In a saucepan, bring raisins, water, juice, and cinnamon to boil. Reduce heat to medium; cook and stir for 15 minutes or until almost all liquid is absorbed. Remove from heat; set aside. Punch dough down and knead 1 minute. Divide dough in half. Roll each half into a rectangle; brush with egg. Spread half of the filling over each rectangle to withing ½ inch of edges. Roll up in jelly roll style; pinch ends to seal. Place each loaf upside down in a greased loaf pan. Cover and let rise until doubled; takes about an hour. Bake at 350 until light golden brown.

Banana Bread

2 C. Flour	2 Eggs
1 C. Sugar	¼ C. Buttermilk
½ C. Margarine	½ tsp. Salt
4 Bananas, ripe	¾ C. Nuts (optional)
	1 tsp. Baking Soda

Blend eggs, sugar, margarine, buttermilk, and bananas together. Add in flour, salt, baking soda, and nuts if desired. Mix well. Pour into greased and floured pans. Bake at 350 until toothpick comes out clean.

Grandma's Date Nut Bread

3 C. Flour

2 ½ C. Pitted Dates, cut up

2 C. Boiling Water

½ C. Sugar

2 Eggs

2 T. Butter, melted

2 tsp. Baking Soda

2 tsp. Vanilla Extract

$\frac{1}{8}$ tsp. Salt

1 C. Chopped Nuts

Pour boiling water over dates and mash. Mix well and set aside. Mix baking soda, sugar, eggs, vanilla, slt, and butter together. Add in flour, dates, and water, adding the nuts in last. Mix well. Pour into greased and floured loaf pans. Bake at 350 until toothpick comes out clean.

Pumpkin Bread

1 ½ Pumpkin (2 15 oz. cans)   1 tsp. Baking Soda
2 ⅔ C. Flour   ½ tsp. Salt
1 ¼ C. Sugar   ½ tsp. Nutmeg
¾ C. Oil   ½ tsp. Ground Clove
½ C. Water   ½ tsp. Baking Powder
3 Eggs   1 C. Nuts (optional)
1 tsp. Cinnamon   1 C. Raisins (optional)

Blend flour, baking soda, cinnamon, nutmeg, clove, sugar, baking powder, and salt together. Mix well and make a well in the mixure. Add in oil, egg, water, and pumpkin. Mix well. Fold in nuts/raisins if desired. Pour into greased loaf pans. Bake at 350 until the center of loaf is not sticky to the touch.

Gingerbread

2 ¾ C. Flour	1 C Butter, melted
1 C. Boiling Water	2 tsp. Baking Soda
1 C. Sugar	1 tsp. Ground Ginger
1 C. Molasses	1 tsp. Salt
2 Egg	1 tsp. Cinnamon

Blend sugar, flour, ginger, salt, cinnamon, and baking soda together. Add in egg, molasses, butter, and water. Mix well. Pour into two greased loaf pans. Bake at 350 until a toothpick comes out clean.

Sweet Corn Bread

1 C. Corn Meal	½ C. Shortening
1 C. Milk	1 Egg
1 C. Flour	3 tsp. Baking Powder
½ C. Sugar	1 tsp. Salt

Cream egg, shortening, milk, and sugar together. Add in corn meal, flour, baking powder, and salt. Mix well. Pour into a greased square or round pan. Bake at 350 until toothpick comes out clean.

Sourdough Starter

1 envelope Active Dry Yeast   2 C. Flour
1 C. Water

Mix yeast, water, and flour together in glass container. Cover with plastic wrap. Leave in warm room for 48 hours. Stir 2-3 times. Batter will ferment, bubble and acquire a slightly sour smell. Makes 3 cups.

To use starter:
Stir batter. Pour off as much of the starter the recipe requires. Add to remaining starter equal parts of flour and water. 2 cups should remain in starter. Stir then let stand for a few hours utnil it bubbles again. Cover and refrigerate.

By replenishing the starter with flour and water, you can keep it going continuously. Never add anything other than flour and water to starter pot.

Sourdough Bread

Bread Machine Recipe

2 C. Bread Flour   2 tsp. Sugar

$\frac{2}{3}$ C. Sourdough Starter   ¾ tsp. Salt

½ C. Water   1 ½ tsp. Active Dry Yeast

Use Bread setting: Basic/Specialty with the light bread color setting on to prevent overbrowning of loaf.

Add sourdough starter and water to pan. Then add flour, sugar, and salt. Tap pan to settle dry ingredients. Level ingredients in pan. Push some ingredients into the corners. Make a well in the center of ingredients and add the yeast. Lock pan into maker. Start bread machine. When bread is done, turn off machine and remove bread from pan. Cool on rack and slice.

Sourdough French Bread

1 ½ C. Sourdough Starter	2 T. Sugar
1 C. Warm Water	2 tsp. Salt
5 C. Flour	1 pkg. Active Dry Yeast

Dissolve yeast in warm water for about 5 minutes. Stir in starter and sugar. Gradually add in 4 C. Flour mixed with salt. Cover bowl with damp towel. Let rise for 1 ½ hours in a warm room. Turn dough onto floured board. Work in 1 C. Flour until dough is no longer sticky. Knead dough until satiny. Shape dough into 1 large round or 2 long oval loves. Set on baking sheet sprinkled with cornmeal. Let rise again in warm place for 1 ½ hours. Put shallow pan of water on lower shelf of oven. Preheat oven to 400. Make diagonal slashes in bread, preferably with razor blade so dough does not fall. Bake for 40 to 50 minutes or until crust is medium dark brown. Set on rack to cool.

Sourdough Biscuits

2 C. Sourdough Starter   1 T. Sugar
1 C. Whole Wheat Flour   2 tsp. Baking Powder
1 C. Flour   ½ tsp. Salt
½ C. Butter

Mix flours and baking powder together. Cut in sugar, salt, and butter. Mix well to make a bread crumb looking dough. Stir in starter. Turn dough onto floured board. Knead lightly; working in flour if very sticky. Roll out to ½ inch thick. Cut into 2 ½ inches in diameter. Place on lightly oiled baking sheet. Let rise in warm place for an hour. Bake at 350 until light brown.

*If using white flour, reduce starter to 1 $\frac{2}{3}$ cups.

Sourdough Pancakes

2 ¼ C. Flour   3 Eggs
2 C. Warm Water   2 T. Sugar
1 C. Sourdough Starter   2 T. Oil
$\frac{1}{3}$ C. Milk   1 tsp. Baking Soda

Mix starter, water, and flour together. Cover bowl; let stand over night. With a whisk beat in eggs, sugar, oil, milk, and baking soda. Let batter stand 10 minutes. Using a hotter griddle than usual, make silver-dollar sized pancakes, using 1 T. batter for each. Flip cake when surface bubbles form.
Mix

Scones

4 C. Flour   5 T. Unsalted Butter
½ C. Milk   2 T. Sugar
1 Egg, beaten $\frac{1}{8}$ tsp. Salt

Mix sugar, flour, and salt together. Cut in butter. Mix to soft dough with milk and egg. Mixture should be slightly sticky, not dry. Roll out ½ inch thick and cut into diamonds, triangles or circles. Bake at 350 until light brown. Serve with butter or jam.

Life's Recipe
-Author unknown-

1 C. Good Thought
1 C. Kind Deeds
1 C. Consideration for Others
3 C. Sacrifice for Others
3 C. Forgiveness
2 C. Well Beaten Faults

Mix these thoroughly and add tears of joy and
sorrow and sympathy for others.
Flavor with little gifts of love.
Fold in 4 cups of prayer and faith to lighten other ingredients
and raise the texture to great height of Christian living.
After pouring all this into your daily life, bake well
with the heat of human kindness.
Serve with a smile.

Dixie's Donuts

3 C. Flour   2 tsp. Baking Powder, heaping
1 C. Sugar   1 tsp. Vanilla Extract
½ C. Milk $\frac{1}{8}$ tsp. Nutmeg
2 Eggs $\frac{1}{8}$ tsp. Salt
2 T. Butter, melted

Mix flour, baking powder, sugar, salt, and nutmeg together. Add eggs, butter, milk, and vanilla. Mix well. Heat oil in pan. Take balls of dough and make into the shape of a donut. Fry dough until brown and set on paper towels to drain. Sprinkle with powdered sugar or cinnamon/ sugar mixture or use a glaze over the hot donuts.

Cinnamon Rolls & Maple Bars

Bread Machine Recipe

2 C. All Purpose Flour	¼ C. Sugar
1 ¼ C. Milk	1 Large Egg
1 C. Bread Flour	1 ½ tsp. Salt
¼ C. Shortening	1 ½ tsp. Fast Rise Yeast

Add ingredients into the pan, except yeast. Level the ingedients in pan. In the center of ingredients, make a well to add the yeast in. You only want to make the dough, not cook it in the machine. Dough will be soft.

For Cinnamon Rolls

Extra Ingredients

Butter, melted   Cinnamon/Sugar Mixture

Roll the dough out into a rectangle to about an inch thick. Brush melted butter onto the dough. Add the cinnamon/sugar mixture. Roll the dough in a tube shape. Slice into 1 ½ inch slices. Place on a baking sheet about 2-3 inches apart. Let sit to raise for one hour. Bake at 350 until golden brown. After the rolls have cooled a little, use the Powdered Sugar Glaze (p. 89) on top.

For Maple Bars

Roll the dough out into a large rectangle to about an inch thick. Cut dough into rectangles for bars or doughnut shapes. Place cut dough onto waxed paper and let rise for one hour. Fry in hot oil. Cool bars/doughnuts then frost with Maple Frosting (p. 89).

Dark Chocolate Walnut Brownies

1 Cube Butter = ½ C. softened or melted

1 ¼ C. Sugar	**1 tsp. Vanilla Extract**
¾ C. Flour	**¼ tsp. Salt**
⅓ C. Dark Baking Cocoa	**½ C. Walnuts, chopped**

Blend butter, sugar, vanilla, salt, and cocoa together. Add in flour and walnuts. Mix well. Pour into a lightly greased 8 inch by 8 inch baking pan. Bake at 350 for 30 minutes and sides are firm to touch.

*This a chewy brownie and a toothpick will not come out clean. Do not add any baking soda.

Candy

Divinity

Grandma's Divinity

2 C. Sugar	1 tsp. Vanilla Extract
½ C. Corn Syrup	1 tsp. Powdered Sugar
½ C. Water	$\frac{1}{8}$ tsp. Salt
2 Egg Whites	½ C. Nuts (optional)

Bring sugar, syrup, water, and salt to boil, stirring until sugar dissolves. Cook to hard ball stage/260 degrees. Meanwhile, beat egg whites until stiff. Pour hot syrup mixture into eggs a little at a time. As candy begins to hold shape add in vanilla, powdered sugar, and nuts if desired. Mix well. Pour into a buttered pan or drop by teaspoon onto waxed paper.

To make flavored divinity:

Chocolate: Blend in **1 C. Chocolate, melted** at the last mixing stage.

Swirled flavors: 1 C. of whatever you are adding: Cherries, mint, etc. Pour divinity into pan then swirl flavor mixure into divinity without mixing it up.

Turtles

1 pkg. Kraft Caramels
Pecan Halves   **1 tsp. Water**
Gharadelli's Chocolate Melting Wafers

Place four pecans in a cross shape with ends meeting. Melt caramels with water. Drop with teaspoon onto center of pecans. Let cool. Melt chocolate per instructions. Cover caramel with chocolate.

Chewy Chocolate Caramels

2 C. Sugar
1 C. Corn Syrup
1 C. Evaporative Milk
$\frac{2}{3}$ C. Baking Cocoa

½ C. Margarine
½ C. Water
1 tsp. Vanilla Extract
$\frac{1}{8}$ tsp. Salt

Blend syrup, sugar, cocoa, salt, milk, and water in a pan. Cook on medium heat, stirring constantly until it reaches 245 degrees. Remove from heat. Stir in margarine and vanilla.Mix well. Pour into a buttered pan. Let cool then cut into squares.

Pecan Logs

7 ½ C. Powdered Sugar	3 pkg. Kraft Caramels
7 oz. jar Marshmallow Cream	2 tsp. Vanilla Extract
1 C. Margarine, softened	1 tsp. Salt
1 C. White Corn Syrup	Chopped Pecans

Blend margarine, syrup, salt, and vanilla together well. Add in sugar and marshmallow cream. Knead until well blended. Make into 1inch by 4 inch logs. Wrap in waxed paper and freeze until set. Melt caramels. Roll logs in the caramel until well coated then in the pecans.

*Any chopped nut can be used.

Honey Candy

2 C. Sugar	1 C. Cream
2 C. Honey	1 stick Butter

Blend sugar, honey, cream, and butter in a 3 qt. saucepan with the sides heavily buttered. Heat mixture slowly, stirring constantly. Cook to 270 degrees. Remove from heat. Pour into a buttered baking sheet. Let cool until it's easy to handle. Butter hands then gather candy into balls. Pull candy until golden and becomes hard to pull. Cut into bite-sized pieces.

O'Henry Bars

4 C. Rice Krispies	12 oz. pkg. Chocolate Chips
1 C. Peanut Butter	1 pkg. Miniature Marshmallows
½ C. Butter	
12 oz. pkg. Butterscotch Chips	

Cook chips, butter, and peanut butter over low heat until melted together. Pour over a blended mixture of rice krispies and marshmallows. Put into a loaf pan. Refrigerate then cut into squares.

No Cook Fondant

3 ½ C. (1 lb.) Powdered Sugar   1 tsp. Vanilla Extract
⅓ C. Margarine, softened   ½ tsp. Salt
⅓ C. White Corn Syrup

Blend margarine, syrup, salt, and vanilla together. Add sugar. Knead until mixture is smooth and well blended.

Peanut Butter/Chocolate Fondant Logs

1 batch No Cook Fondant   Peanut Butter
Chocolate, melted   Nuts (optional)

Roll out fondant to about ¼ inch thick. Spread peanut butter/chocolate/chocolate-nut mixture over fondant evenly. Roll up like a jelly roll. Chill. Slice rolls in ½ inch sections, making pinwheels.

Chocolate Dipped Bonbons

1 batch No Cook Fondant   Flavored extract
Food Coloring   Chocolte, melted

Add flavoring &/coloring to fondant batch. Roll into balls and chill.
Dip set balls in chocolate for bonbons.

Peanut Logs and O'Suzie's

1 batch No Cook Fondant   **3 pkg. Kraft Caramels**
Peanuts   **Chocolate, melted**

Make fondant into 1 inch by 4 inch logs. Wrap in waxed paper and chill until set. Melt caramels with a teaspoon of water. Roll fondant logs in the caramel until well coated. Roll in peanuts.

For O'Suzies, dip peanut logs in melted chocolate.

Chocolate Covered Cherries

60 Maraschino Cherries
2 C. Powdered Sugar
3 T. Margarine

3 T. Light Corn Syrup
1 ½ lbs. Dipping Chocolate

Drain cherries and place on paper towel. Blend margarine, syrup, and salt together. Stir in sifted powdered sugar. Shape1 tsp. of the sugar mixture around each cherry. Place on waxed paper-lined baking sheet. Chill. In a heavy saucepan, melt chocolate, stirring constantly. Do not add any liquid. Spoon chocolate over cherries or dip balls into the chocolate. Store in a covered container.

Recipe for Friendship

Take two heaping cups of Patience,

One heartful of Love,

Two handfuls of Generosity,

A dash of Laughter,

One headful of Understanding,

Sprinkle generously with Kindness,

And plenty of Faith, and mix well.

Spread over a period of a Lifetime,

And serve everybody you meet.

Chocolate Peanut Clusters

1 small pkg. Ghiradelli Dark Chocolate Melting Wafers
12 oz. pkg. of Beer Nuts

Melt chocolate per instructions. Shake excess salt off of the nuts. Blend chocolate and nuts together. Drop into candy cups or onto waxed paper in cluster shapes.

*Flavors will vary depending on nuts used.

English Toffees

English Toffee

1 C. Butter	2 T. Water
1 C. Sugar	1 tsp. Vanilla Extract
¾ C. Nuts	$\frac{1}{8}$ tsp. Salt

Cook butter, sugar, water, and salt together on medium heat until 305 degrees. Stir occasionally. Mixture will become dark, remove from heat and stir in the vanilla. Stir vigorously. Pour and spread out mixture onto a buttered baking sheet. Sprinkle with chocolate chips. As chips melt, spread over toffee. Sprinkle top with nuts. Cool over night.

*Do not refrigerate.

*Chocolate chips can be any flavor.

*Instead of nuts, dried raisins or cranberries can be used instead.

Chocolate Suckers

2 C. Sugar

1 C. Corn Syrup

1 C. Evaporative Milk

$\frac{2}{3}$ C. Baking Cocoa

½ C. Margarine

½ C. Water

1 tsp. Vanilla Extract

$\frac{1}{8}$ tsp. Salt

Blend syrup, sugar, cocoa, salt, milk, and water in a pan. Cook on medium heat, stirring constantly until it reaches 250 degrees. Remove from heat. Stir in margarine and vanilla. Mix well. Pour into a buttered candy molds and add sticks. Let cool.

Peanut Butter Fudge

3 C. Sugar

⅔ C. Evaporated Milk

7 oz. jar Marshmallow Cream

12 oz. pkg. Peanut Butter Chips

¾ C. Peanut Butter

1 tsp. White Corn Syrup

1 ½ Stick Margarine

Cook sugar, milk, and margarine together in heavy sauce pan on medium heat. Stir constantly until mixture comes to a boil. Boil for 5 to 7 minutes. Remove from heat. Add in chips, peanut butter, and 1 tsp. syrup. Mix well then add marshmallow cream. Mix well. Pour into a buttered pan. Let cool and cut into squares.

Nut Brittles

2 C. Sugar	1 tsp. Vanilla Extract
1 C. White Corn Syrup	1 tsp. Baking Soda
½ C. Water	$\frac{1}{8}$ tsp. Salt
1 T. Butter	1 lb. Nuts

Cook sugar, syrup, and water on medium heat. Stir until sugar is dissolved. Cover with lid. Boil for 3 minutes. Remove cover. Cook without stirring to 250 degrees. Warm nuts in microwave for a minute. Add nuts, stirring constantly. Cook until brittle reaches the 305 degrees. Add in the baking soda and salt. Stir vigorously. Pour onto buttered baking sheet. Spread out. As brittle cools, lift and pull with metal spattulas and forks, separating nuts and thinning the candy.

*Brittle can be made in these, plus other flavors:
    Cashew-Macadamia-Coconut
    Sunflower Seed-Smoked Almond
    Mixed Nut
    Add Jalapenos, drained over night to any brittle
*Candy will be at 300 degrees so you do not want to touch it.
*This recipe has been in our family for over a 100 years.
*Any nut brittle can be dipped in melted chocolate for a different taste.

Grandma Cornman's Hard Candy

3 ¾ C. Sugar   1 C. Water

1 ½ C. Light Corn Syrup   5-6 drops Food Coloring

1 T. Flavoring Extract or 1 tsp. Flavoring Oil

In 2 qt. pan, mix sugar, syrup, and water. Cook at medium heat, stirring constantly, until mixuture is boiling. Boil without stirring until mixture reaches 310 degrees. Remove from heat, add extract/oil and coloring. Pour onto foil covered generously with powdered sugar. Cool and break into pieces.

*Can also be poured into buttered candy molds.

Chocolate Fudge

3 C. Sugar   7 oz. jar Marshmallow Cream
1 ½ Sticks Margarine/Butter   1 tsp. Vanilla Extract
$\frac{2}{3}$ C. Evaporated Milk   12 oz. Chocolate Chips

Cook sugar, margarine, and milk over medium heat, stirring until sugar dissolves. Cook while constantly stirring until candy reaches 236 degrees. Remove from heat. Add vanilla and chocolate chips. Mix well and mix in marshmallow cream. Mix in chopped nuts if desired. Pour into buttered pan. Let stand until set.

*Any flavored chocolate chip can be used.

*Any 1 C. chopped nut can be added as well.

This
&
That

Popcorn Balls

½ C. Sugar   ¼ C. Oil
½ C. Popcorn   2 T. Butter
½ C. Corn Syrup   ½ tsp. Salt

Pop popcorn in air popper or use natural flavored microwavable popcorn. Put popcorn into bowl. Boil sugar, syrup, salt, and butter, stirring until it's mixed well and mixture is boiling. Pour mixture over popcorn. Shape into balls with buttered hands. Mixture will be hot.

Caramel Popcorn

6 to 10 qts. Popped Corn
2 C. Light Brown Sugar
1 C. Butter
½ C. White Corn Syrup
1 T. Molasses

1 T. Vanilla Extract
1 ½ tsp. Salt
½ tsp. Baking Soda
1 to 2 C. Peanuts (optional)

Keep popcorn in oven to keep warm. Cook butter, syrup, sugar, and salt together. Boil 5 minutes on low heat; do not stir. Remove from heat. Stir in soda and vanilla quickly. Pour mixture over the popcorn and nuts, if desired. Coat popcorn well. Bake at 250 for 1 hour, stirring every 15 minutes. Cool on wax paper.

Sweet Roasted Cinnamon Almonds

¼ C. Sugar   2 T. Water
1 C. Almonds   2 tsp. Cinnamon

Cook sugar, water, and cinnamon together. Add almonds. Stir constantley until no moisture remains. Pour out onto foil lined baking sheets.

Sweet & Spicy Pecans

2 C. Pecan Halves   ½ tsp. Cinnamon
¼ C. Brown Sugar   ¼ tsp. Nutmeg
2 T. Margarine   ¼ tsp. Salt
1 T. Water

In a 2 qt container, microwave margarine for 30 seconds. Stir in brown sugar, cinnamon, nutmeg, salt, and water. Mix well. Stir in pecans until the sugar mixture coats the nuts. Microwave, uncovered, on high for 4 to 5 minutes, stirring every minute. Spread nuts onto a baking sheet. Separate any nut stuck together and let cool.

Candied Pecans

1 C. Nuts   ½ tsp. Salt
½ C. Brown Sugar   ¼ tsp. Corn Syrup
¼ C. Water

Cook all ingredients on medium heat until it boils. Stirring constantly. Pour onto baking sheet. Bake at 325 for 15 minutes.

Party Mix

3 C. Corn Square Cereal   6 T. Butter
3 C. Rice Square Cereal   2 T. Worcestershire Sauce
3 C. Wheat Square Cerial   1 ½ tsp. Seasoned Salt
1 C. Mixed Nuts   ¾ tsp. Garlic Powder
1 C. Pretzels   ½ tsp. Onion Powder

Heat oven at 250. Melt butter in a large roasting pan in oven. Stir in seasonings. Gradually stir in cereal, nuts, and pretzels until evenly coated. Bake for 1 hour, stirring every 15 minutes. Spread on paper towels to cool. Store in airtight container.

Ranch Snack Mix

1 pkg. Miniature Pretzels   ¾ C. Oil
2 pkg. Bugles   1 can Salted Cashews
1 envelope Ranch Dressing Mix
1 pkg. Bite-sized Cheddar Cheese Fish Crackers

In two large bowls, combine pretzels, Bugles, cashews, and crackers. Sprinkle with dressing mix; toss gently to combine. Drizzle oil over mixture. Toss until well coated.

Fudge Frosting

3 T. Milk   ¼ C. Margarine

3 T. Cocoa   1 tsp. Vanilla

3 C. Powdered Sugar

Boil the milk, cocoa, and margarine for one minute. Add in the powdered sugar and vanilla. Mix until well blended.

Powdered Sugar Glaze

1 C. Powdered Sugar   2 T. Milk

2 tsp. Vanilla Extract

Blend all ingredients together. Add tablespoons of powdered sugar to get a thicker glaze.

Maple Frosting

3 C. Powdered Sugar   2 T. Maple flavoring

½ C. Milk

Blend all ingredients together. Mix well.

Decorator Frosting

1 C. Shortening

1 lb. Powdered Sugar

¼ C. Egg White

2 T. Butter, softened

2 T. Cornstarch

1 tsp. Vanilla Extract

Using an electric mixer, beat shortening and butter until smooth. At low speed, add 2 cups powdered sugar, ¼ cup at a time. Then add cornstarch. Beat at medium speed until mixed well. Beat in remainder of powdered sugar until mixture is smooth and stiff peaks form when batter is raised. Cover bowl and refrigerate.

Cream Cheese Frosting

1 lb. Powdered Sugar

8 oz. Cream Cheese

½ C. Butter

¾ C. Nuts/Raisins (optional)

2 tsp. Vanilla Extract

Combine ingredients until frosting is smooth.

Fluffy White Frosting

1 ½ C. Sugar	2 tsp. Light Corn Syrup
½ C. Water	1 tsp. Vanilla Extract
2 Egg Whites	$\frac{1}{8}$ tsp. Salt

In top of a double boiler, combine egg whites, sugar, salt, water and syrup. Put over boiling water and beat with mixer for 7 minutes or until stiff peaks form. Blend in vanilla.

Chocolate Buttercream Frosting

2 ¾ C. Powdered Sugar	½ C. Baking Cocoa
$\frac{1}{3}$ C. Milk	1 tsp. Vanilla Extract
½ C. Butter, softened	

Cream butter then add cocoa and sugar alternately with milk. Beat until spreading consistency is reached (additional milk may be needed). Blend in vanilla. Mix until smooth.

Pie Crust Mix

3 lbs. Shortening   **1 ½ T. Salt**
16 C. Flour

Blend shortening, flour, and salt together. Mix well. When ready to bake, mix 1/3 C. water to 2 C. of the mix to bake your crust. Roll out dough and then cover pie pan and cut to shape. Pinch edges to top of pan. Bake at 350 until light brown. Crust is ready for filling.

Crumb Pie Crust

1 C. Graham Cracker Crumbs   **2 T. Sugar**
$\frac{1}{3}$ C. Butter, melted   **½ tsp. Cinnamon**

Blend cracker crumbs, sugar, cinnamon, and butter together. Mix well. Pat mixture into the bottom and sides of a pie pan. Chill before filling or bake at 350 for 10 minutes.

Pie Filling

2 C. Dried Fruit   Water   Sugar

Place fruit in pan. Add water until it covers the fruit. Add sugar to taste. Boil filling until fruit is tender.

Cream Cheese

1 C. Cottage Cheese   1 T. Lemon Juice
3 T. Milk

Blend ingredients together adding milk and juice one tablespoon at a time until mixture is smooth.

Mayonnaise

1 ½ C. Oil   2 tsp. Salt
3 Egg Yolks   1 tsp. Ground Mustard
3 tsp. Vinegar

Whisk yolks and other ingredients together, adding oil to reach the right thickness. Texture varies from store bought.

Condensed Milk

1 C. Dry Milk	$\frac{1}{3}$ C. Boiling Water
$\frac{2}{3}$ C. Sugar	3 T. Margarine, melted

Blend all ingredients together in a blender. Beat until smooth.

Powdered Sugar

1 C. Sugar   2-4 T. Cornstarch

In blender, process sugar until very fine. Add cornstarch and process further.

Brown Sugar

2 T. Molasses   1 C. Sugar

Blend molasses and suagar together with fork. Store brown sugar in a canister to keep it soft.

Dog Maple Syrup Cookies

5 C. Whole Wheat Flour $\frac{2}{3}$ C. Milk
3 C. Flour   4 Eggs
2 C. Maple Syrup   1 tsp. Salt
1 ½ C. Shortening   1 tsp. Vanilla Extract

Mix all ingredients together. Roll out dough. Cut into strips or shapes. Cook as is or put a thin layer of maple syrup or sugar on top. Bake at 350 until sides are golden brown.

Dog Biscuits

1 C. Whole Wheat Flour   ½ C. Oats
$\frac{1}{3}$ C. Shortening   ¼ C. Yellow Cornmeal
¾ C. Nonfat Dry Milk Powder   1 Egg
½ C. Flour   1 tsp. Sugar
½ C. Water   1 T. Chicken/Beef Bouillon Granules

Combine flours, powder, oats, cornmeal, and sugar together. Add in shortening until mixture becomes coarse crumbs. Stir in egg. Dissolve bouillon in water then add into mixture. Stir with fork and form dough into a ball. Knead on floured board for 5 minutes. Roll dough until ½ inch thick. Shape into biscuits. Put on plate and microwave for 5-10 minutes or until dry and firm to touch.

Index

Apple Crisp......................................12

Banana Bread...............................46

Banana Oatmeal Cookies....................37

Brown Sugar..................................94

Butterscotch Pudding........................19

Candied Pecans...............................87

Caramel Popcorn............................85

Carrot Cake..................................15

Cheese Cake..................................14

Chewy Chocolate Caramels..................65

Chocolate Butter Cookie....................21

Chocolate Chip/Candy Cookies.............31

Chocolate Chip Oatmeal Cookies..........38

Chocolate Covered Bonbons...............69

Chocolate Covered Cherries................71

Chocolate Covered Peanut Clusters.........73

Chocolate Cream Frosting...................91

Chocolate Crinkle Cookie..................21

Chocolate Divinity.......................63

Chocolate Fondant......................69

Chocolate Fudge.........................82

Chocolate Marshmallow Drops.........40

Chocolate Peanut Clusters...............73

Chocolate Pudding......................18

Chocolate Shortbread Cookies...........28

Chocolate Suckers.......................76

Chocolate Sugar Cookies................23

Cinnamon Oatmeal Cookies............36

Cinnamon Regfridgerator Cookies......24

Cinnamon Rolls.........................58-59

Condensed Milk.........................94

Cream Cheese...........................93

Cream Cheese Frosting..................89

Crumb Pie Crust........................92

Dark Chocolate Walnut Brownies........60

Decorator Frosting......................89

Devil's Food Cookies....................34

Divinity.................................63

Dixie's Donuts............................57

Dog Biscuits.............................95

Dog Maple Syrup Cookies................95

Easy Pound Cake.........................16

English Toffees.........................75

Fluffy White Frosting..................91

Fried Pies..............................13

Fudge Brownie Pie.......................17

Fudge Frosting..........................89

Ginger Bread............................49

Ginger Snaps............................26

Grandma Cornman's Hard Candy.........81

Grandma's Date Nut Bread..............47

Honey Candy............................67

Life's Recipe...........................56

Maple Bars............................58-59

Maple Frosting..........................89

Marian's Chocolate Sheet Cake...........9

Mayonnaise..............................93

Melting Moments.........................24

Mom Hudson's Apple Dump Cake............12

No Bake Cheese Cake.........................15

No Bake Cookies...............................35

No Bake Fruit Cake............................16

No Cook Fondant...............................69

Nut Brittle.......................................79

O'Henry Bars...................................67

Old Fashioned Coffee Cake....................10

Oreo Cookie Dessert..........................20

Party Mix..88

Peacan Logs.....................................66

Peacan Pie.......................................17

Pecan Sandies...................................28

Peanut Butter Cookies.........................32

Peanut Butter Fondant.........................69

Peanut Butter Fudge...........................78

Peanut Logs & O'Suzie's.......................70

Pie Crust Mix...................................92

Pie Filling..93

Pinwheel Galaxy Cookies......................33

Popcorn Balls   84

Powdered Sugar...........................94

Powdered Sugar Glaze...................89

Pumpkin Bread...........................48

Christmas Pumpkin Cake................11

Raisin Bars & Muffins....................43

Raisin Bread............................45

Ranch Snack Mix........................88

Recipe for Friendship...................72

Rolo Cookies...........................39

Scones..................................55

Shortbread Cookies.....................27

Snickerdoodles..........................30

Sourdough Biscuits......................54

Sourdough Bread.......................52

Sourdough French Bread................53

Sourdough Pancakes....................55

Sourdough Starter......................51

Sugar Cookies..........................22

Sweet & Spicy Pecans...................87

Sweet Corn Bread   50

Sweet Roasted Cinnamon Almonds.........86

Tea Cakes...................................25

Thumbprint Cookies.......................29

Turtles.......................................64

Vanilla Pudding...........................19

Vanilla Wafers..............................35

Wacky Cake..................................8

Made in the USA
Columbia, SC
28 November 2022